Mad
Parade

Mad Parade

Neil Fulwood

STACK
BOOKS

Smokestack Books
1 Lake Terrace, Grewelthorpe, Ripon HG4 3BU
e-mail: info@smokestack-books.co.uk
www.smokestack-books.co.uk

ISBN 9781739772215

Smokestack Books
is represented
by Inpress Ltd

in memory of Bill Hicks

'*A week is a long time in politics.*'
attrib. Harold Wilson

'*All governments are lying cocksuckers.*'
Bill Hicks

Contents

God Save Your Mad Parade

Deluge-drenched, they line the Mall,
grateful for discomfort. They're in thrall
to the iron fist in the velvet glove.
They'd kneel gladly and call it love.

The iron fist in twin set and pearls
and Ascot hat. The flag damply unfurls.
Uniforms, ribbons, medals and robes -
throwbacks to Britannia ruling the globe.

Street parties hosted by those who vote Leave,
Little England clutching at reasons to believe.
Parochialism buttered up by the WI,
pomp and a big fat circumstantial lie.

God save the Queen, the Church and the State,
God smite those the establishment hate,
God bless Buck House and the Royal Mint,
God bless every cheap liar in Parliament.

And God bless the sheep still lining the Mall,
God bless the delusion placating them all,
God grant for Saxe-Coburg-Gotha's sake
that none of their subjects suddenly wake.

June 2016

Thoughts & Prayers

Thank you for choosing thoughts & prayers.
Before using thoughts & prayers for the first time
please read the following guidelines. Thoughts
& prayers should be deployed only during times
of tragedy or national mourning. Thoughts & prayers
are unsuitable for small-scale incidents,
unfortunate accidents or bad luck. Thoughts
& prayers are not to be activated privately –
the manufacturer's guarantee will be invalidated
unless sound bite or news camera footage
can demonstrate media-appropriate usage.
It is recommended that thoughts & prayers
are kept in a locked cabinet, wrapped
in oilcloth. You can obtain spare cartridges
of thoughts & prayers from your local retailer.
All thoughts & prayers are government-approved.

June 2016

Lines Thought to Have Been Written on the Eve of the Publication of the Chilcot Report

Yea, though I walk through the shadow
of 2.6 million words, I will fear
no impeachment. The raiments
of legalese enfold me.

The word shall be proclaimed
as promised by Rupert.
Lo! the smokescreen of headlines.
Lo! the great dimming of memory.

Bow your heads, my children
and repeat the catechism:
'acted with the best of intentions...
information available at the time.'

Tomorrow I will coat myself in snake oil
and smile for the cameras.

July 2016

The Love Song of Tony Blair

WMD – that's a nice acronym
I'll be with you whatever
Saddam Hussein – let's topple him
I'll be with you whatever

Fill the news with anger about I-raq
I'll be with you whatever
We've got the guns and each other's back
I'll be with you whatever

We've got the missiles, the tanks, the planes
I'll be with you whatever
All those oilfields waiting to be drained
I'll be with you whatever

The ground troops ready to be deployed
I'll be with you whatever
We'll sort the dead from the men and the boys
I'll be with you whatever

For God and country and Lockheed Martin
I'll be with you whatever
For approval ratings and profit margins
I'll be with you whatever

July 2016

Three Ring Circus

The clown isn't funny anymore:
the face-paint and fright wig
have seen to that – the leering
smear of orange. Now there are clowns
on the streets of every major city
and some have knives and none smile
and balloons aren't their stock-in-trade.

The woman on the flying trapeze
isn't so dazzling now; her manoeuvres
have become conservative, her eye
at all times on the safety net.
Her husband, the former circus master,
applauds from a seat in the shadows:
the sound of one platitude echoing.

The ticket price is ruinous. Entry
depends on photo ID. Tawdry bunting
is watermarked with messages
from both their sponsors. The strongmen
wear uniform free of insignia. Sit quietly.
applaud when you're told. The human
cannonball has been trained on the crowd.

November 2016

An Address to Beelzebub

in rebuttal of his attempt to overshadow Burns Night by installing Donald J Trump in the White House

I woke this morning, careworn, sick,
Dreams haunted by the rhetoric
Of a presidential speech (its schtick
       Bombast, hot air)
Delivered by a lunatic
       With ugly hair.

He says he'll make the country great,
Believes he's been ordained by fate
But how can he hope to heal when hate
       's polluting
His words and those of his best mate,
       Vladimir Putin?

Some think he's Russia's puppet Prez,
Some cite conflicting interests
And deem his close alliances
       Depraved, necrotic.
But all of that's untrue, he says:
       He's patriotic.

Buy American only, he explains,
To boost the dollar's rate of exchange.
And yet the labels remain the same
       On the designer
Shirts and ties of his signature range:
       Made in China.

But this is a man who stacked up tall
A brickwork of promises – a wall –
And none of them mean bugger all:
   The guy's two-faced.
Plain facts do the job of this doggerel
   And state the case.

But facts are things for him to fritter,
Tear up, discard, flush down the shitter.
Political spin is blinged-up glitter
   While facts are nude.
Repeat a lie enough on Twitter,
   You'll make it true.

When even Facebook proves too broad
As canvas for the written word,
Is the pen's resilience to the sword
   Now in retreat?
Is the only message that strikes a chord
   A lousy Tweet?

A hundred-and-forty character limit's
Unconducive to the message within in
Yet those in a war of words seek to win it
   With an epithet
Worth less than a flyer the moment you bin it
   Or a deleted text.

So where to look for nuance and depth,
Objectivity and analysis?
Don't rely on the mainstream press
   To undermine
The elite when career journalists
   Just toe the line.

Big business backs the candidate
Who's willing and able to fulminate
Against what the voter's told to hate
        By sloganeering,
Who promises to make things great
        And gets 'em cheering.

But the morning after's cold and grey
And regret's the order of the day
As promises get stowed away,
        Not made good on.
Small hands conduct the state of play,
        Hands there'll be blood on.

Beelzebub: for what it's worth,
The hour's not yours, though hope's in dearth
And anger lubricates the mirth
        Of this standard habbie –
To hell with you and your minions on earth.
        I'll drink to Rabbie!

January 2017

Singing a Happy Song

'There's no wheels on my wagon
But I'm still rolling along...'
Bob Hilliard

It might seem kind of scary moving forward on our own
but Theresa May's in office and Liz is on the throne,
there'll be jobs for all us Brits again and fish 'n' chips for tea –
don't worry, sing a happy song, we'll Brexit breezily.

There'll be bulldogs barking Britishly on every cobbled street,
there'll be cheerful Cockney urchins and bobbies on the beat,
there'll be Spitfires zooming overhead doing victory rolls –
don't worry, sing a happy song, God bless all British souls.

We'll have a great big party now we've got our country back,
we'll do a dad-dance, have a fight, salute the Union Jack,
we'll all get drunk and bolshy, go out immigrant-bashing –
don't worry, sing a happy song, racism's in fashion.

We'll act like it's the 70s (just without the industry),
we'll get to speak our mind again and it'll all be non-PC,
nobody will be offended when every Briton's white –
don't worry, sing a happy song, everything's all right.

The streets will all be clean and safe, the buses run on time,
we'll channel our inner Churchill like it's 1939,
it's us and them, we'll win the day then have a cricket match –
don't worry, sing a happy song, there'll be no turning back.

Free movement's now restricted, but why leave home again?
(except for our six-monthly hols: timeshare out in Spain.)
Well maybe not this year since the pound just took a dive –
but don't worry, sing a happy song, it's good to be alive.

Britain's red, white and blue again (with a dash of purple/yellow)
So let's get down the pub, lads, and I'll buy a round of Stella;
Oh shit, that's foreign, innit? It's back to pints of bitter –
don't worry, sing a happy song, we'll all get pissed much quicker.

Democracy. The people spoke. So don't make any fuss.
Let's work to take this country back to how it never was.
Britain's skies are blue again, Europe's cold and grey –
don't worry, sing a happy song, everything's okay.

March 2017

The First Hundred Days: A Summary

'Day one we're gonna build the wall,
Scrap Obama's policies, one and all,
Thirty days and ISIS will fall' –
        Or so he said.
He talked plenty big but didn't walk tall;
        Went golfing instead.

He fired some missiles at a landing strip,
A man with small hands on a temper trip,
Gave the order to let some hardware rip
        'Cos he got mad.
Didn't stop planes taking off from it.
        Loser. Sad.

He dropped a dirty great bomb on Afghanistan
Which 'probably' killed a handful of men
Who because they lived near a cave system
        Must have been ISIS.
Well, that's terrorism roundly defeated then!
        (I'm taking the piss.)

His dick-swinging contest with Vladimir P
Played out in public, embarrassingly.
When bromance devolves to frenemy
        Should one mention
(Pass me a rhyming dictionary)
        The sexual tension?

Let us not speak of North Korea,
How Donnie brought us too bloody near,
His Bay of Pigs Re-enactment gear
        Awaiting the codes.
Two nutjobs with egos and really bad hair
        Going toe-to-toe.

Or rather, in Donnie's case, tweet to tweet,
Since that's the arena where he finds his feet.
When thousands of fools retweet every bleat
       The big lie prevails.
The truth and Breitbart – the twain shan't meet;
       Integrity ails.

Though he'll still conduct interviews
Guaranteed to give transcribers the blues
Wherein grammar and syntax, dead of misuse,
       Find themselves buried
Under screeds that leave the reader confused;
       Yugely, very.

God knows what goes through his toupee'd head
When every word-mangled sentence he's said
Can't be trusted, checked or taken as read
       As all sense is lost.
But look on the bright side: we're still not dead.
       Fingers crossed.

June 2017

Zero Training Value

'Spokesman Thomas Mills told the BBC: 'From a Navy standpoint, we do hold our aircrew to the highest standards and this is absolutely unacceptable. It has zero training value and the aircrew is being held accountable.'
BBC News website, 17 November 2017

It's *Top Gun* meets *American Pie*:
A rather large willy contrailled in the sky.

Smaller or saggier, you'd be tempted to laugh
But these US flyboys don't do things by half –

A Boeing Growler has decked heaven's halls
With a whopping great whang and a small pair of balls.

What possesses the crew of a military jet
To get hard on the sky: a dare or a bet?

Is it a comment on the state of the nation,
Congenital over-compensation?

Self-expression, completely unfettered?
The mother of all resignation letters?

As the sky-dick goes viral to media mirth,
The top brass are fuming: there's no training worth

In creating a phallus way up in the clouds.
Articles of conduct say that ain't allowed.

But is there a reason that nobody's reckoned?
Does an unsheathed sky-dick offer protection?

If fighters zoomed over from North Korea
They'd tug their joysticks and turn tail in fear

Rather than look a willy that big in the face.
A star-spangled stiffy protecting airspace!

Oh say can you see it, resplendent and big?
Back off Russkies with your Kamovs and MIGs.

All hail the sky-dick till the contrails fade,
O'er the land of the free and the home of the brave.

November 2017

Paint It, Blue

after the Rolling Stones

I see a passport and I want its cover blue.
Don't care if England's eco-nom-ic-ally screwed.
I see people checking in with passports burgundy,
It's a colour too close to red for a true-blue Brit like me.

I see a line of Brits all waiting for a plane
With passports bluer than the azure skies of Spain.
I see people shake their heads, another long delay,
Post-Brexit this kind of shit just happens every day.

I look inside my passport, not that many stamps,
I need a piss-break and my leg has got the cramps,
Maybe I'll just go home and not visit Tenerife.
What d'yer mean it serves me right because I voted Leave?

I wanna see my passport
Covered blue
Blue as the sea
Blue as loneliness
See Europe
Blotted out by stupidity

I see my passport and it's now all nice and blue,
I'm not going anywhere, but my lion-heart is true,
You'll see me queuing up, dressed in my Converse shit,
If it gets my country back then I'll stand and wait a bit.

December 2017

The Apprentice Bard

Some titled toff called Alan Sugar
thought he was being a clever bugger
slagging off Corbyn in end-stopped rhyme –
Christ, his metrics were a punishable crime.

No wit, no nuance, no technique
(no surprise if you've heard the shyster speak) –
just bile, bilge and barrow-boy rabbit
and a racist remark about Dianne Abbott.

Foaming at the mouth, old Sugar is sour
that a socialist is the man of the hour,
so he claims Corbyn scorns our forces' dead
when he'd rather not have them killed instead.

Sugar's rage: the ember of a dying flame,
a shit TV show the half-life of his fame:
a scowl and a face like a dreich bank of mist,
the finger of a struck-off proctologist.

He's still got the Roller and the custom suits
but it's been untold years since his firm produced
a product that wasn't pie-in-the-sky,
that even a UKIP supporter would buy.

'Yesterday's man,' says Shug of JC –
this from the guy whose Amstrad PC
was cutting edge back in Eighty-Six.
Has he done owt since then? Big fucking nix!

April 2018

Harry and Yanny and Meghan and Laurel

Laurel hangs bunting and arranges balloons
in bunches of red, white and blue
while Yanny tots up the cost of the celebrations
and cuts funding to front line services.

Laurel sets out place mats with crown motifs
and double checks the seating plan
while Yanny moves on anyone not wrapped
in a flag or clutching official merchandise.

Laurel gets teary-patriotic drunk
and gasps at the dress
while Yanny takes a Stanley knife
to the sleeping bags of the homeless.

May 2018

On the Occasion of President Donald J Trump's State Visit to the United Kingdom

To the sceptre'd isle came Don the Dumb;
No sooner deplaned from Air Force One
Than he gave an interview with *The Sun*
　　　And flapped his trap:
Said a US-UK deal wouldn't be done
　　　Or some such crap.

Bile and rhetoric: Don's favourite groove:
A particularly unstatesmanlike move.
The mainstream media raised the roof
　　　And howled the blues.
Don's predictable lie was hitched to a truth:
　　　The Sun – fake news.

Don does denial when facts come tootin',
Wouldn't know the truth if it came out shootin'
Or cosied up closer than Big Vlad Putin,
　　　His bud-cum-pimp.
Look to the skies and try disputin'
　　　The Trump baby blimp.

Behold the dirigible; its praises sing!
Laud and applaud it as it takes to the wing,
Filled with all the hot air of the real thing.
　　　The likeness is epic:
It's rotund and orange and everything!
　　　Just less dyspeptic.

Peaceful protest at its sharpest and finest,
Satire at is most accurately unkindest,
The baby blimp designed to undermine his
　　　Spoiled brat squalling.
The dirigible's a masterpiece of the childish
　　　But its muse is appalling.

So get back on the plane, Donnie my lad,
You'll not get from us what you get from Vlad.
Your hair's a disgrace and your tweets are sad.
        We'll do owt to spite ya.
We didn't make the final, best not make us mad –
        We'll fucking fight ya.

July 2018

Boris: A Spotter's Guide

See Boris. Boris has a shit haircut.
Boris looks like Donald Trump
only less orange. Looking like Donald Trump
is a bad look for anyone. Even
Donald Trump. Boris thinks women
in the burqa look ridiculous.

See Boris. Boris dresses like a banshee
on crystal meth would dress if it lived
in a house without mirrors and didn't have
a best friend to be brutally honest
with it. Boris thinks women
in the burqa look ridiculous.

See Boris. Here's Brexit Boris in a photo
wearing a safety sling like a nappy
and gurning like a bad imitation
of Benny Hill. He's wearing a crash helmet
and waving a flag. Boris thinks women
in the burqa look ridiculous

because Boris is happy to pass comment
on other people's dress, just as Boris
is happy to laugh at 'piccaninnies'
and pump the oil of casual racism
onto waters refugees have drowned in.
But it's all right because it's Boris, innit?

August 2018

Britain-Fest

Britannia's pawned her trident and her shield,
both flecked with rust, they didn't fetch much brass.
The British lion's fucked off to some far field,
to dream nostalgic dreams in veldt-like grass.

It's 2022: fried rat and tripe's
the national dish; we're fighting over scraps.
It's slowly coming home to John Bull types
that Brexit Britain's fifty shades of crap.

We're out of Europe, crippled by the bill,
and no-one wants to buy what we don't make.
Britannia's mangy lion is dreaming still
and crown and state dislike the word 'mistake'.

The MayBot's will be done: a grand event
to set the doubters' doubting tongues to rest.
Pomp and glory: a statement of intent.
Something Victorian. A Britain-fest!

So roll up, folks, roll up. Come one and all,
help celebrate this septic isle's story.
The latest chapter's likely to appal,
full of UKIP pricks and boorish Tories.

The main enclosure's decked out to the max,
'made in Taiwan' flags and Poundland bunting.
Here's Nigel Farage clutching pint and fag.
What dozy tosser let that rotten...

Moving swiftly on, the Rees-Mogg tent is
open for tea and monocle repairs.
A pale sideshow freak ex-*The Apprentice*
is spouting racist bilge, but no-one cares.

Theresa's Big Top Circus fails to thrill,
the Johnson tent ensheaths a floppy dick,
folk stumble off the Gove Train looking ill
or chuck away their fried rat, feeling sick.

Prince William's due on soon. He's followed by
a fly-past of the RAF's last planes
(a huge formation V-sign in the sky)
and then a marching band unless it rains.

There's more joy at a violent *coup d'état*
or Christmas spent with turkeys while they're plucked
than this damp squib that's Brexit's last hurrah:
the Festival of Britain Now We're Fucked.

October 2018

Meaningful

The guy behind the counter is loosing off smoke rings.
The vape shop is empty but for him
and those half dozen perfect, useless circles.

On the street, the cold makes dragon's breath
of my exhalations. Tomorrow's 'meaningful vote'
has been called off. I've pulled my neck into my collar,

found holes burying my hands in my pockets.
Five minutes' walk to the pub and I'm wondering
if the mood will be muted or murderous

or if anyone still cares.

December 2018

Your Flight Has Been Delayed Due to a Convenient Media Distraction

The magic bus, that hellbound train,
a horse once ridden by John Wayne,
balloonatics eight miles high,
ghost riders in the freakin' sky,
the Flying Dutchman cursed to roam,
Gatwick shut down by a drone.

Theresa's deal dead cert to fail,
cue phoney outrage (*Daily Mail*)
re: what Corbyn said or didn't say ...
oops, here's more bad press for May:
if it's not Brexit vote hesitation,
it's the white paper on immigration;

meanwhile a vote of no confidence
hints that Corbyn might quit the fence.
Sturgeon's ready to get in the ring –
IndyRef2, bad-a-fuckin'-bing!
Cable and Lucas are hoisting the sales
and there's a new kid on the block in Wales.

But don't worry about any of that,
here's a drone flown by some silly prat
who Sussex police and the army can't catch.
Arrivals and departures – scratched!
Holidaymakers – shit out of luck!
Christmas breaks are royally fucked.

This is England (you'd never have guessed)
and the hardest nuts in the SAS
and the Paras' deadliest crack-shots
can't take down a boy-toy some wanker got
from Argos, Curry's or the Range.
Maybe I'm cynical, but ain't that strange?

December 2018

Plan B

Observe. A statue of Christ is helicoptered
in Fellini's *La Dolce Vita* to St Peter's Square.
Meanwhile, in an unproduced screenplay,
a chopper buzzes over the unsexy sprawl
of Grantham bearing an effigy of Thatcher
away from the awayday mob who organised
and travelled and turned up to tear it down.

Keep watching. The entire special effects budget
is about to blow chopper and statue to hell.
Panavision's finest from a dozen angles
have the fireball covered. The footage
is an editor's wet dream, inviting montage,
slo-mo, the full bag of film-making tricks,
the image repeated into iconography.

Let it go. None of this was ever shot. None
of those who deserved it were ever shot.
Che's just a screenprint on the bedroom wall
of a student getting his end away to Nicki Minaj.
The revolution was kicked to the kerb,
social justice pause-buttoned in favour
of a night down the pub and a dirty kebab.

Plan B. A smattering of blue heritage plaques
to mark the murkiest moments of those
who govern us. This is where a shiny suit
bet the country on a losing hand.
This is where a tweed jacket sank a pint
and smirked and bleated about immigrants.
This is where a buffoon with a Union Flag

dangled from a wire like a Poundland Bond.
These are the not-so-big boys who did it
and ran away. And this is the z-grade
Thatcher tribute act clutching the hot potato
as if it were the Holy Grail, endlessly parroting
'The thing means the thing means some
weak approximation of the thing.' And this

is Parliament where the whole edifice is crumbling
even as it takes back control. Placards
jink above the crowds outside. MPs post selfies
from the 'No' lobby. This is Parliament and these
are our honourable friends. This is where
it all went to hell. This is where it all went to hell.
This is where it all went to hell. This is where it all

January 2019

Poem on the Relevance, Integrity and Political Impact of Change UK/The Independence Party

April 2019

Tommeh

after Rudyard Kipling

He picketed a courthouse to politicise a trial,
a bargain basement bigot whose ways and means were vile.
He played the lone reporter with some breaking news to probe
but the truth is Tommeh Robinson's a sad Islamophobe.
O it's Tommeh this and Tommeh that and Tommeh Robbo's tops
but he's Stephen Yaxley-Lennon to his mum and to the cops.
To his mum and to the cops, boys, to his mum and to the cops,
O he's Stephen Yaxley-Lennon to his mum and to the cops.

He toured the streets of Warrington, preaching words of hate,
when a milkshake left its paper cup to spatter on his face.
He lunged for his attacker, fists swinging Billy-O
while looking like an outtake from a dodgy video.
O it's Tommeh this and Tommeh that and Tommeh does the biz
but it's Stephen Yaxley-Lennon wiping off the lactose jizz.
Wiping off the lactose jizz, boys, wiping off the lactose jizz,
O it's Stephen Yaxley-Lennon wiping off the lactose jizz.

He went into a polling booth to see his name writ down,
dead sure the other candidates were all a bunch of clowns.
He swaggered like a brash young man out sowing wild oats
but his lower lip was trembling when they counted up the votes.
O it's Tommeh this and Tommeh that and vote vote vote for Tommeh
but it's Stephen Yaxley-Lennon whose deposit's up the Swanee.
His five grand's up the Swanee, boys, his five grand's up the Swanee,
it's Stephen Yaxley-Lennon whose deposit's up the Swanee.

May 2019

The Day May Resigned

after Frank O'Hara

It's 2pm in England, Friday, a bank
holiday weekend looming and the weather
unEnglishly glorious. I've pulled an early swerve
after a debrief on my professional competence
and I'm thinking of getting a pint, maybe at Langtry's
or Yarn, and watching the pretty young things
strut their studied indifference. There are good days
and bad days, you roll with the punches. There's a cliché
for every occasion. I could go somewhere with a juke,
feed it a quid and blast some Chumbawumba,
see who joins in with *I get knocked down but I get up again.*

I could take my afternoon off, buy it a bucket of popcorn
and watch a movie. But is three hours of *deus ex machina*
enough to sway me from the simple pleasure of a pint
and wasted time? Oh, wasted time: a wanker sign
angled in the direction of clock face, calendar, the human
        construct
of time itself. A birdie flipped at every prison-yard second
ticking away from here to retirement. I could waste my time
in so many ways this afternoon. But I end up
sticking my hand out for a bus and going home.

I haul washing out of the machine, peg it on the line.
Lob cans and bottles in the recycle bin. Iron shirts for work
next week. I throw mozzarella and vine tomatoes
in a ciabatta, break out the pesto. There's a beer in the fridge.
While I'm eating, I noodle on the iPhone; check the news.

You're gone and it's not like things will get better.

May 2019

The Masque of Anarchy (Remix)

for AH

'If you fight, you won't always win.
But if you don't fight, you will always lose.'
Bob Crow

1.
As I worked my day job in Nottingham
I tried to convince myself I didn't give a damn
Any more: it was all too absurd, too vile.
Then a voice urged me to walk another mile.

2.
I met a cold-hearted liar on the way,
Grinning the viperish smile of Esther McVey:
Empty soundbites and a tombstone wave
And all the warmth of Thatcher's grave.

3.
Seven plague rats scurried in her wake
Like the grimmest of images from William Blake:
By their saw-sharp teeth, permanently rent,
The guiltless flesh of the innocent
Was suffered to suffer till the rats were spent.

4.
Next came Fraud, the straw-haired fop,
Who'd have marched at the head, but a photo op
Distracted him and he played the fool –
A bumbling joker whose joke is on you.

5.
And the little acolytes who bowed at his feet
And declared their loyalty was complete,
Dead sure that Boris was a dead cert with voters
Forgot their fave was a lapdog to POTUS.

6.

Armed with a Bible and a copy of Penthouse
The excrescent blob installed in the White House
Became a filthy, priapic, slobbering mess
At the thought of fucking over the NHS.

7.

But more homunculi were playing havoc
Much closer to home: I saw Sajid Javid
Buy his way into the Society of Posh White Lads
With a policy that would have deported his dad.

8.

I saw Dominic Raab, chinless Brexit prince,
Re-handed the reins of incompetence.
Give him a map, ask him, 'Where's Calais?'
And he'll blame his failure on Theresa May.

9.

Priti Patel came marching: right right right,
A cut-throat Zionist Thatcherite
And a poster-girl for hypocrisy and cant,
Forgetting she's the daughter of an immigrant.

10.

I queried morality of Andrea Leadsom:
She bluntly replied, 'You're better off dead, son.
I was a city banker, I'm in favour of fracking.'
I wrestled with rhymes while she walked off laughing.

11.

Gavin Williamson walked a zig-zag line,
A former Remainer who thinks Brexit's fine,
A former staunch supporter of May
Who's u-turned real quick in support of BJ.

12.
This pageant's ranks of not-great-and-not-good
Was swelled by the after-thought of Amber Rudd,
A career MP who's achieved less than nothing,
The cabinet version of an eggless McMuffin.

13.
The parade continued, grimmer and sillier:
Truss and Barclay and Hancock and Villiers,
Sharma and Smith, Jenrick and Shapps,
Jack, Cairns and Buckland. Who gives a crap?

14.
But then it occurred: was not caring about them
The grand slimy plan of the flop-haired PM?
It was easy to glance at the long list of names
And miss two big hitters from the Wall of Shame.

15.
Nicky Morgan, empress of the serpentine,
Who'll sign up to any heartless party line;
So long as she's in with the ruling class,
You can kiss the after-image of her ass.

16.
And then there's the cad who acts like a cove,
The bilious and villainous Michael Gove,
A man who looks like Pob gone evil,
The genetic offspring of snake and weevil.

17.
I watched them march in their serried ranks
And images struck me of armed men and tanks
And curfews enforced and billyclub beatings
And bad decisions made in secret meetings.

18.
I saw truth, Trump-ravaged, making an exit.
I saw Johnson get hard over no-deal hard Brexit.
I saw gleeful hands rubbed in gentlemen's clubs
As victory was achieved in Wetherspoons pubs.

19.
I saw a nation bisected by hate,
Half claiming a Tory as their new best mate.
I saw reason, truth and common sense
Tried and hanged without evidence.

20.
Maybe we'll rise like lions or fighters,
Incensed at the injustices that betide us.
We are many and they are few,
But they own the cops, the banks and the news.
Fight with the fist, the keyboard or pen.
As the man said: you won't always win,
But if you don't, you will always lose.

August 2019

Sonnet in the Time of Meh

The news is in re: Labour leadership
(strangely enough, the Murdoch press seems calmer):
ladies and gents – no martial brass lets rip –
let's hear it for, ahem, Sir Keir Starmer.
There was a time when this would be my cue
to write an epic poem, take the piss,
but though locked-down there's better things to do;
it's a bind just to sit here writing *this*.
Could it be my fighting spirit's dead
or Covid-19's left me feeling blighted?
FFS, the people's party led
by a lawyer who's (shoot me now) been knighted
and all I want's to shrug and turn the page
when I ought to be consumed with fucking rage.

April 2020

Milquetoast Paradise

after Coolio

As I walk through the chamber where they hold PMQs,
I take a look at myself and get the Red Tory blues
'Cos my dynamic with the government's what forklifts are to lorries,
I enable Big Dom Cummings and the UK's best mate, Boris.
But I ain't never abstained without a good reason,
Could've had BoJo on the ropes, swung a punch, left him bleeding
But I watch what I'm saying, don't do too much opposing,
My homies watch the ratings and the numbers are closing.
I really hate to preen, but the BBC
And *The Guardian* got nice things to say about me.
I'm the Labour leader all the little centrists wanna be like,
On my knees looking pious for the media spotlight.

Been spending all my time
Living in a milquetoast paradise.
Made my rep getting hard on crime
Living in a lawyer's paradise.
Now I'm a centrist in my prime
Living in a milquetoast paradise.
I treat the Left like dirt or slime
Living in a milquetoast paradise.

The worst government we've seen facing Covid-19
Disregard their own advice, Cummings drives to test his eyes
But I gotta be down with the blue team,
'Critically support' them while I chase the dream
So I puff myself up till I burst at the seams
And the press say I'm 'forensic' like they know what it means.
I'm no different from the Tories, doing everything Blair meant ta,
And I'll fire any muthafucka who drifts left of centre.
A ratings lead ain't but a headline away
So play the game, do the same, do what I say.
I ghosted out BLM live on BBC
'Cos floating Tory votes are all that matter to me.

Tell me why you Lefties just can't see
That you're worth the shaft for my victory.

NHS getting privatised?
I'm living in a milquetoast paradise.
My predecessor victimised?
I'm living in a milquetoast paradise.
BoJo's bootlickers hypnotised?
I'm living in a milquetoast paradise.
I should be fighting for human rights
But I'm living in a milquetoast paradise.

Ratings and approval, approval and the ratings,
Strong showing in the polls and no-one berating.
Keeping feathers unruffled till the next election,
Even Laura Kuenssberg slips me easy questions.
Critics say I'm dull, but I'm sly like George Smiley,
Getting righteous Tweets from Oberman and Riley.
You think I'm doing nothing, trying to play it cool,
But I'm planning two terms of Tory-lite rule.

Gonna win and spend my time
Living in a milquetoast paradise.
Sell the unions down the line
Living in a milquetoast paradise.
A purge on the Left sounds just divine
Living in a backstabber's paradise.
Deflecting Tory bad press 'cos I'm
Living in a milquetoast paradise.

Tell me why you Lefties just can't see
That you're worth the shaft for my victory.

June 2020

Good Riddance

When it's broken, throw it on the dump.
Throw it out on its ass, its heinie, its rump.
Acknowledge its vacuity. Let it stump
future generations that such a waxen lump
of nothing could gain office, could pump
those in its spider-like grip into a clump
of echo-chamber fiends. Imagine a sump
draining out its clogged fluids: *whoomp!* –
a match ignites the septic mess. Jump
back, watch it burn. It's gone. Fist bump!

November 2020

Traurigverliererdämmerung

Hark! The overture's Wagnerian –
Germanic, Teutonic, Bavarian,
Dour as a Scots presbyterian,
        Dreary and grey,
Each new chord a scary 'un,
        Dies irae.

But whose *dies* are we *irae*-ing?
Surely now it goes without saying
That Republicans are baying
        At the hiding
They took from GOP-slaying
        Harris and Biden.

So imagine how DJT feels,
The crown prince of the dirty deal
Who never won but had to steal,
        Day one to present.
He can't believe this is real.
        He's effervescent.

Act one begins. Hoist the curtain.
Int. Oval Office. Donnie's certain
That if he spends enough time blurting
        He's the winner
The press will stop their flirting
        With the thinner,

More photogenic, non-fake-tanned
Democrat whose calm, statesman-
like persona's bound to command
        The world's attention.
Don ensures the flames are fanned
        By gross contention,

Calumny, cant and outright lies.
Truthful journos? Damn their eyes!
A cynical and seditious surprise
  Is what he's plotting:
Watch as democracy's compromised
  By something rotten.

He launches lawsuits against the states
Where the Biden-Harris turnout's great
And gives the nod to his bezzie mate
  R. Giuliani
To go forth, rant, gesticulate
  And plain act barmy.

It's pure *Carry On*: Rudy's best shot
At press engagement's the parking lot
Of a landscaping firm some lackey got
  Mixed up with a chain
Of luxury hotels who, TBH, are not
  Dissimilarly named...

Except Four Seasons hotels don't tend
To favour locations shared with low-end
Adult bookstores, where the view of a crem
  Isn't aesthetic;
And the sight of Rudy gone round the bend
  's truly pathetic.

'Allllll the networks,' Rudy declares
And madly waves his fists in the air;
Pomaded sweat seeps down from his hair,
  His eyes are hazy
As if he were drunk, otherwise impaired,
  Or just plain crazy.

Act two. Here's Don addressing a crowd,
Barking instructions good and loud
To Anonymous Qs, Boys who are Proud
   And the easily led.
He says he's beleaguered but unbowed.
   He makes 'em see red

Then looses 'em, hounds off the leash
Slavering, barking and baring their teeth;
Throws the stick of his hate at democracy
   And urges them on,
Says he'll march with them. But look – see –
   He fucks off home.

To Capitol, then, they come *en masse*:
Here's one with their firm's ID pass
Visible; here's another silly ass
   Dressed as a Viking;
A MAGA mob who think it's a gas,
   Their Twitter feeds spiking.

Live-streaming in high resolution,
Telling journos it's a revolution,
Pretty much handing the prosecution
   A watertight case.
(That laughter coming in ghostly dilution
   's from Lenin's grave.)

One puts their feet on Pelosi's desk,
One nicks a laptop to sell to the Reds,
All use their phones, unaware the Feds
   Can triangulate signal.
Then it's over. Broken windows. Some mess.
   Sad bastards. Dismal.

Act three (Jeez, no intermission?)
Sees Donnie clarifying his position
Re: inciting rioters to sedition
            (He claims he didn't)
While MAGA muppets facing prison
            Want pardons written.

As if he's realised how far up
Shit Creek his leaky boat is stuck
And how, paddle-wise, he's out of luck,
            Donnie agrees
To quit being a whiny little fuck
            And hand the keys

To the office he grossly profaned,
Mocked, debased and smeared with shame
For the four years of his wretched reign,
            To Forty-Six;
But he still can't bear to say Biden's name,
            The mardy prick.

And during these final fleeting days,
What does defeated Don have to say?
Are his fulminations a riotous affray,
            Bilious and bitter?
Who knows. His platform's been taken away
            By FB and Twitter.

Thus act three stumbles to its end:
From Camelot's ruins Don descends,
Devoid of honour, legacy, friends –
            A shyster most foul.
This is the way the presidency ends,
            Not with a coup but a scowl.

January 2021

Great Lost Episodes

1 Good Ole Boys

In the great lost episode of *The Dukes of Hazzard*
the corrupt and corpulent Boss Hogg sends
bumbling sheriff-cum-errand-boy
Roscoe P. Coltrane out of town to collect
some dodgy PPE while he refines a plan to rid
Hazzard County of them pesky Duke boys
(both parts played by Keir Starmer, one live action
the other rendered in slightly bland and plastic
CGI – IMDb is kinda coy as to which is which).
Things get into high gear when Bo and Luke Duke
accidentally stumble on the PPE consignment,
figure out they could use it to disgrace Boss Hogg
in front of the town council, and instead hightail
back to the farm to drink moonshine and strum
the banjo – because that, friends, is how folks in
Hazzard County abstain. With thirty-five minutes
of screen time still to fill, Boss Hogg gets caught out
dealing unregulated pharmaceuticals, Roscoe
P. Coltrane fluffs a media interview (hilarity ensues)
and the Duke boys go burning down the abstention
turnpike so damn fast they trigger a speed trap.
The script calls for Bo and Luke to drive a 1969
Dodge Charger, but due to some unrecorded
production error the episode features a Hillman Imp
nicknamed the Pink Flag. During the obligatory car chase,
the Pink Flag tries to avoid a burning clown car
with Boss Hogg at the wheel. (The missing scene
which explicates this plot development
has yet to resurface). Tyres squeal, dust is kicked up
in asthmatic quantities and there's some energetic
steel guitar. The car chase ends with Boss Hogg
managing to steer the clown car over a cliff edge
while the Duke boys discover the bridge over the creek
is washed out. The Pink Flag could easily make the jump
in a crowd-pleasing stunt but Bo and Luke abstain.

2 The Fat Controller

In the great lost episode of *Thomas the Tank Engine and Friends*,
the Fat Controller (voiced in earlier seasons by David Cameron,
since the reboot by Boris Johnson) waddles from disaster
to disaster as he tries to privatise the Isle of Sodor's railways.

Jeremy the Socialist Engine is bricked up in a disused tunnel
after spelling FUCK DOCTOR BEECHING in huffs of steam
whilst standing at a station where a horde of *Daily Mail* readers
are waiting for a train with blue paint and good old-fashioned

Sodor values, thank you very much, not this goddamn commie
loco. His run is reassigned to Keir the Bland Engine. Mean-
while, Priti the Nasty Engine is busy identifying all the little
engines who don't have 100% Sodor-made parts, and shipping

those who don't back to wherever they were built. That they hauled
goods and passengers to the benefit of Sodor's economy
for decade after decade doesn't mean a damn thing. This
is the kind of steam-whistle politics that grabs the headlines –

and the voters by their fireboxes. Look how much traction
Nigel the Septic Tank gained from it – and he's not even
an engine! (Though he has been seen coupled to the gravy train.)
Mid-episode, Priti the Nasty Engine's behaviour raises some issues

over bullying, while the Diesels Matter Too campaign snowballs.
The Fat Controller commissions an inquiry into institutionalised
diesel-ism on Sodor's railways and makes damn sure
the results won't offend any of his steam loco base.

Diesel-ism doesn't exist, the Fat Controller declares, breezily
going back to fucking up the timetables and downsizing
the menu in the waiting room cafe. The token diesel
on the investigatory panel resigns in disgust. Unrest ignites

into riots. A statue of Sodor's first railway baron is pulled down
and chucked in the harbour along with a Double-O gauge model
of Priti the Nasty Engine. Signal boxes burn. Choking gouts
of smoke drift over a forgotten siding, tucked away out of sight,

where Keir the Bland Engine, fire doused, is keeping well out of it.

3 Camberwick Greensill

for Rob Kenchington

In the great lost episode of *Camberwick Green*,
the musical box opens in jerky stop motion:
can you guess what is in it today? It's PC Starmer.
Hello, PC Starmer, number 452

[the mono-expressive bobby gives a slow
almost hesitant wave], how are you today?
[Frown; roll of the eyes.] Is something wrong,
PC Starmer? [Nod.] Oh dear... This goes on

for a good five minutes, then there's a song
about PC Starmer's forensic methodology.
TV shows were slower paced back then.
Long story short, it's come to PC Starmer's

attention that Windy Miller
has been lobbying for a lucrative contract
at Pippin Fort. Captain Snort
has a history of handing out contracts

to old buddies rather than going to tender
in the approved manner, and trousering
the kickbacks. The episode was probably
pulled because of the word 'trousering'

(it's funny how things work at the BBC);
certainly the scenes of Windy Miller
drinking cider with Sergeant Major Grout
wouldn't have raised an eyebrow

when the show debuted. Possibly
the coded phone call Windy makes
to Mr Honeyman – who keeps
the treasury – might have been confusing

to younger children. Or it could have been
the lack of resolution to the episode:
PC Starmer asks Captain Snort to conduct
a full and open investigation into corruption

at Pippin Fort, Captain Snort fobs him off
with something along the lines of 'no need
to go public with any of this, I'll just have
a quick word with the lads and clear up

any misunderstandings, you toddle off
back the station and have a jam doughnut,
all right?' – which, admittedly, is difficult
to convey in wordless stop motion.

The episode ends with PC Starmer
looking a bit sad as he disappears back
into the musical box, when it should have been
that slippery bastard Windy Miller going down.

4 Sometimes You Want to Go...

In the great lost episode of *Cheers*
Frasier Crane struggles to disabuse
dimwit barman Woody of his Covidiot
opinions; misunderstandings reach
a crescendo with the appearance
of special guest star Keir Starmer
who is promptly ejected from the bar.
Live studio audience response
was muted, with only a running joke
about Keir Starmer being called Keith
(Cheers: where nobody knew his name)
generating more than low-grade titters.
The episode was shelved. Keir Starmer
never returned to the venue.
His career in comedy has since been
confined to PMQs and LBC phone-ins.

April 2021-July 2021

Canticle for a Racist

After he died
they all but renamed the pub
The Hagiographers' Arms.

That corner seat
which to hear him talk
was the last true seat

of untainted Englishness
has now the feel of a shrine
where a candle flickers against

but never quite burns
a list of nationalities
he'd not have had sit there.

That torrent of unfounded hate
the first pint unleashed –
you'd have thought he'd held forth

with the moral purpose
of St Thomas Aquinas or
Mother Theresa.

The way the regulars
speak of him now
he might have been royalty.

April 2021

'When I Went out into that Garden'

When I went out into that garden
I saw plants and trees and grass
and a bunch of civil servants
of good breeding, stock and class;
and as I took a few more steps
'neath the sunlit firmament,
I looked at the lack of work being done
and thought 'this is a work event'.

When I went out into that garden
to glad-hand and to schmooze,
I carefully ignored the makeshift bar
and the suitcase full of booze;
and if a glass was in my hand,
then it wasn't for me it was meant
because I was only there as their leader
to look in on a work event.

When I went out into that garden
no-one told me I shouldn't be there
so I walked around and pressed the flesh
and languidly took the air;
I'd issued some guidance earlier,
urged the police force not to relent
in curtailing illegal gatherings
(free pass for a work event).

When I went out into that garden
where people were milling around,
glasses and bottles amassing,
fag ends strewn on the ground,
I never thought I'd be sowing
the seeds of such vicious dissent
or that an investigation
would look into this work event.

So here's what I know of the garden:
it was an office annex of sorts;
nobody told me not to be there
or how much booze had been bought.
I apologise quite profoundly
for the rules I deny that I bent,
I was barely even there, you know,
at the garden par – ... uh, event.

January 2022

They Will All Take Us with Them in the End

after Tom Lehrer

When you click into your news app
it's not comforting that what's hap-
penning out there is global brinkmanship.
Europe's status quo's been ballsed up
by a goon who wants to call up
every missile that he's got and let them rip.

But don't you worry.

No more Tory lockdown scandals,
no more guff about Prince Andrew,
or price hikes, NHS, or student debt;
if BoJo, Biden and Vlad P
push this shit past DefCon 3,
you won't care about bent coppers in the Met.

'Cause they will all take us with them in the end,
when diplomacy's been fucked off round the bend
and a jab of that red button
vends total world destruction –
you'd be 'MAD' not to know how this one ends.

They will all take us with them in the end,
loudly claiming they had something to defend.
Was it a patch of foreign soil
or the current price of oil?
Did the Footsie close ahead right at the end?

Oh they will all take us with them to the grave,
telling lies about the lives they tried to save.
There'll be no more cant and spin
with the planet all done in
and no world leaders left to rant and rave.

Down by the old maelstrom,
Liz Truss is wondering what went wrong.

And they will all drag us down with them in flames,
with no scapegoat left behind to take the blame.
We'll finally be united
when that fireball's ignited,
nearly eight billion unrecorded names.

They will all drag us down to dust and ash,
the victims of an act both cruel and rash,
dead as some assassin's mark
care of a pissed off oligarch
deprived of his wads of laundered cash.

Of course they'll take us with them in the end,
they'd do the same if they had their time again,
so hum a Missa Solemnis
just before that Yellow Sun hits
and the farewell bash concludes at Number Ten.

You will all go directly to your version of heaven.
There will be no hero to save the day, no 007.

For they will all take us with them in the end,
every man, woman, child, foe and friend.
When history overtakes us
and we all turn slightly vaporous,
yes they all will take us with them,
oh they all will take us with them,
yes they all will take us with them in the end.

February 2022

Notes

God Save Your Mad Parade
Celebrations for the Queen's 90th birthday took place between 10–12 June 2016. The EU referendum was held on 23 June 2016.

Thoughts & Prayers
On 12 June 2016, fundamentalist Omar Mateen killed 49 people and injured 53 others after opening fire at the Pulse nightclub in Orlando. Politicians and pundits earnestly offered their thoughts and prayers but stopped short at any consideration of gun control.

Lines Thought to Have Been Written on the Eve of the Publication of the Chilcot Report
Following a seven-year inquiry, the Chilcot Report into Britain's role in the Iraq War was published. It ran to 2.6 million words across 12 volumes and effectively let Tony Blair off the hook.

The Love Song of Tony Blair
Eight months before the Iraq War, Tony Blair sent George W Bush a memo pledging 'I will be with you whatever'.

Three Ring Circus
American elections always tend towards the showmanship and low-brow antics of the three-ring circus. The 2017 campaign between Democrat Hillary Clinton and Republican Donald J. Trump was a particularly rancorous and vulgar example.

An Address to Beelzebub
Donald J Trump was sworn in as the 45th President of the United States of America on 20 January 2017. With Burns Night, the traditional celebration of Scotland's greatest poet, falling on 25 January, it seemed appropriate to homage his satirical poem 'Address to the Devil'.

Singing a Happy Song
Article 50, announcing the UK's intent to withdraw from the EU, was triggered on 29 March 2017. The Leave campaign had traded in nationalism and flag-waving rhetoric leading to a spike in racially motivated hate crimes in the immediate aftermath of the result. Michael Gove had assured the country in April 2016 that 'the day after we vote to leave, we will hold all the cards and we can choose the path we want'; Liam Fox declared in July 2017 that a post-Brexit trade deal with the EU would be 'the easiest in human history'; and Boris Johnson announced an 'oven-ready' Brexit deal in October 2019.

The First Hundred Days: A Summary
The fact check published on the NPR.org website assessing Trump's pledges for his first hundred days in office in the context of what was actually delivered makes for amusing reading.

Zero Training Value
In November 2017, the crew of a Boeing EA–18G Growler drew a penis in the sky over Okanogan County, Washington, with the jet's contrail. The US Navy failed to see the funny side and disciplinary action ensued.

Paint It, Blue
The replacement of burgundy passport covers with blue ones was trumpeted by Brexiteers as a vindication of their anti-EU ideology. The concession for the new passport covers was awarded to a French firm. File under *irony*.

The Apprentice Bard
Entrepreneur and host of *The Apprentice* Alan Michael Sugar spent much of the 2010s castigating Jeremy Corbyn on social media and making blatantly racist attacks against Dianne Abbott.

Harry and Yanny and Meghan and Laurel
As the nation's flag-wavers and Royalists geared up for the wedding of Prince Harry to actress Meghan Markle, and the homeless were unceremoniously herded off the streets of Windsor, the internet was gripped by an auditory illusion whereby listeners attuned to a higher frequency heard the name Yanny while those more keyed to a lower frequency heard Laurel.

On the Occasion of President Donald J Trump's State Visit to the United Kingdom
Donald Trump's state visit to the UK in July 2018 coincided with England's World Cup defeat. Protests against Trump were widespread. A crowd-funded blimp in the shape of a screaming baby with Trump's face became the defining image of his visit.

Boris: A Spotter's Guide
Shortly after resigning as Foreign Secretary, Boris Johnson drew criticism and accusations of racism for a comment in a newspaper article comparing women wearing the burqa with letterboxes. Johnson shrugged off the issue, despite Islamophobic incidents rising by 375% in the week after the article was published.

Britain-Fest
In September 2018, beleaguered Prime Minister Theresa May announced plans for a Festival of Britain to be held in 2022. The aim was to celebrate national unity following the UK's withdrawal from the EU. Her party was being riven by a civil war conducted around Brexit-defined battle lines, and she would announce her resignation eight months later. File under *irony*.

Meaningful
On 10 December 2018, Theresa May delayed a 'meaningful vote' on the withdrawal agreement with the EU during widespread controversy over the Irish backstop. She delayed the vote again on 24 February 2019. Her Brexit deal was voted down by a majority of 149 on 12 March 2019.

Your Flight Has Been Delayed Due to a Convenient Media Distraction
Sightings of a drone near Gatwick airport led to the cancellation of hundreds of flights between 19 and 21 December 2018. A couple from Crawley were arrested and detained for 36 hours, and subsequently released without charge. On 23 December, DCS Jason Tingley of Sussex Police gave a confusingly-worded statement to the press suggesting that there might not have been any drone activity in the first place. The investigation was closed without resolution 18 months later at a cost to the taxpayer of £800,000.

Plan B
After Theresa May's original Brexit proposal was overwhelmingly voted down, she was given until 21 January 2019 to return to Parliament with a 'Plan B'. She duly presented an only slightly tweaked version of Plan A. Around the same time, it was announced that a statue of Margaret Thatcher, rejected by London, would be erected in her home town of Grantham. Two years later, South Kesteven District Council was still embroiled in controversy and disagreement over the projected £100,000 unveiling costs. *La Dolce Vita* is a 1960 film directed by Federico Fellini about cafe society, tabloid journalism and the trivialities of the rich.

Poem on the Relevance, Integrity and Political Impact of Change UK/The Independent Party
Formed in February 2019 and formally dissolved ten months later, Change UK was made up of a cluster of Labour and Conservative MPs who had resigned from their erstwhile parties. Founding member Chukka Umunna quickly left Change UK to join the Liberal Democrats, managing the hat trick of three different political affiliations between February and June 2019.

Tommeh
Former EDL leader Tommy Robinson was arrested in May 2019 after live-streaming information which threatened to undermine a court case against a grooming gang. He received a short prison sentence. The same month, while campaigning as an independent MEP in Warrington, Robinson was pelted with a milkshake, as was former UKIP leader Nigel Farage in Newcastle.

The Day May Resigned
Frank O'Hara's 'The Day Lady Died', on the death of Billie Holiday, achieves a genuine pathos through its accretion of minutiae. In referencing it to mark the resignation of Theresa May, my aim was to conjure mundanity via the mundane.

The Masque of Anarchy (Remix)
Having ousted Theresa May, Boris Johnson assembled a cabinet of hardcore Brexiteers. My friend A.H. suggested that a new take on Percy Bysshe Shelley's classic call to action 'The Masque of Anarchy' was called for. I took up the challenge.

Sonnet in the Time of Meh
After Jeremy Corbyn stood down as leader of the Labour party, he was replaced by Sir Keir Starmer who debuted a style of opposition based on fence-sitting, abstention and blind indifference to the open goals presented to him by Boris Johnson's rapidly unravelling Tory government.

Milquetoast Paradise
As the Black Lives Matter movement gained traction on both sides of the Atlantic, Sir Keir Starmer ghosted BLM in a BBC interview. He similarly refused to demonstrate solidarity with unions, the LGBTQ+ community and the Palestinian struggle, choosing instead to 'critically support' Boris Johnson's corrupt and cronyist government.

Good Riddance
Donald Trump lost the 2020 presidential election fair and square to Joe Biden. He refused to concede, insisting without a scrap of proof that the result was fraudulent.

Traurigverliererdämmerung
Götterdämmerung, the last opera in Wagner's epic cycle *Der Ring des Nibelungen*, translates as 'Twilight of the Gods'. *Traurig-verliererdämmerung* is cod German, my best attempt at 'Twilight of the Sad Loser'. Trump's final weeks in office were marked by a flurry of lawsuits against pro-Biden states; he incited a mob to storm the Capitol building, lied about his involvement, and finally exited the Oval Office in a sulk, refusing to attend Biden's inauguration.

Great Lost Episodes
For the first few months of 2021, I wrote no political satire; it seemed like the state of the nation was beyond parody. As newsfeeds filled up with the Matt Hancock PPE snafu, the outcome of the trial against protestors who relocated a statue of slave-trader Edward Colston, right-wing voices criticising the BLM movement, and former Tory PM David Cameron's involvement in the Greensill scandal, it seemed like Keir Starmer's Labour Party were being presented with one open goal after another. Starmer, predictably, did nothing.

Canticle for a Racist
HRH Prince Philip, the Duke of Edinburgh, died aged 99 on 9 April 2021. The mainstream press automatically went into hagiography overdrive, recasting a lifetime's worth of unapologetic racism and cultural insensitivity as the hilarious gaffes of a loveable eccentric.

'When I Went out into that Garden'

During a car crash TV interview in January 2022, Boris Johnson was challenged over photographic evidence that he had attended a garden party at 10 Downing Street in contravention of the very COVID rules implemented by his own government. "When I went out into that garden, I thought that I was attending a work event," he claimed. The widely circulated photograph clearly indicates that cheese and wine were being consumed, and that none of the usual administrative or clerical accoutrements one would expect of a work event were present.

They Will All Take Us with Them in the End

On 24 February 2022, Russian president Vladimir Putin authorised military incursion the Ukraine following a long and complex timeline during which tensions had escalated between the Ukrainian government and pro-Russian separatists, a situation not helped by NATO troop deployment. Sanctions were swiftly announced by the UK and US governments, although these achieved very little in quantifiable terms. The media irresponsibly fanned the flames, oversimplifying the conflict to the point of infantilism. Tom Lehrer's *We Will All Go Together When We Go*, a 1959 skit on Cold War anxiety, provided the inspiration for this poem.

Acknowledgements

Several of these poems, or earlier versions of them, have appeared in *I Am Not a Silent Poet, Medusa's Kitchen, Poetry 24, Your One Phone Call, New Boots and Pantisocracies* and *Spilling Cocoa Over Kingsley Amis.*

My thanks to: Liz Baugh, Lucy Beckett, Amy Clarke, Andy Croft, Matt Fox and everyone at the Organ Grinder, Paula Fulwood, Harry Gallagher, Robert Kenchington, Roy Marshall, Louise Newton, Harry Paterson; and to family, friends and comrades.